Chattanooga Writers' Guild

Anthology

Volume VII

Chattanooga Writers' Guild Anthology, volume seven

Copyright © 2022 Chattanooga Writers' Guild
ISBN: 9798218133429

Chattanooga Writers' Guild
2288 Gunbarrel Rd. #154-251
Chattanooga, TN 37421

chattanoogawritersguild.org
facebook.com/chattanoogawriters
twitter.com/chattwrtrsgld
instagram.com/chattanoogawritersguild

Cover art and design by
Michelle Young

Interior layout and design by
Vulgar Scullery Maid Publishing, LLC
vulgarscullerymaid.com

This anthology is dedicated to **Chris Wood**, for all her hard work, enthusiasm, energy, and commitment to the Chattanooga Writers' Guild. Nothing could happen without her, and we are so grateful for everything she does.

"Tennessee Valley Railroad Museum train in 2021"

photograph by Becky Parker

Contents

Foreword

When I moved to Chattanooga in 2015, I was determined to find "my" people. I'd briefly lived here before from 2011-2012, but moved away because I didn't feel a connection to the city or its inhabitants. But Tennessee, and Chattanooga in particular, had settled in my heart, and so I decided to give it another chance. This time I knew I'd have to be more proactive in finding my place in the community. One of the first groups I reached out to was the Chattanooga Writers' Guild.

I joined and became an active member of a critique group, but did not reach out to the greater Guild community for the first year. I had found a few like-minded writers who were willing to help me with my novel-writing attempts, so why should I bother attending the monthly meetings or workshops where I didn't know anyone and probably wouldn't hear anything I hadn't already heard before? I was a former English major, after all.

But then towards the end of my first year as a member, I heard there was a need for people to join the Board. Having been on the Board of nonprofits before, I understood all too well how difficult it can be to find volunteers to fill these necessary positions. And thus I became the Secretary, which allowed me to get to know some of the "old timers" - the people who not only were long-time members, but also had been helping to lead the group for many years. Fantastic, hard-working people like Finn Bille, Sherry Poff, John C. Mannone, Karen Phillips, and Ray Zimmerman.

Then, because I was now a Board member, I thought I ought to start showing up at the monthly meetings - doing my part to welcome people and support the Guild. Right away I was disappointed in myself for not attending these meetings sooner. Every meeting was an opportunity to meet more writers, more people who understood the frustrations, difficulties, conundrums, and joys of this particular artistic endeavor. I also quickly realized that every presenter we brought to our programs had something to teach me. I shake my head when I look back at my arrogance now, and I am thankful that I finally went to a Writers' Guild Monthly Meeting and was given the opportunity to learn new things again.

By becoming more involved in the Guild, I was able to continue creating connections and friendships with such wonderful people as Chris Wood, Mark Anderson, Helga Kidder, Michelle Young, KB Ballentine, Kelly Hanwright, Natalie Kimbell, Ann Thornfield-Long, and Cynthia Young. There's also numerous people I've had the pleasure of speaking with at parties and workshops, people who have stepped up when the CWG needed volunteers, and of course our wonderful writing group leaders who set aside time every month to keep these supportive, welcoming, critique groups going. A big thank you to all of you for all that you do!

I am so proud of all we have accomplished in the six years I have been on the Board, and I have nothing but high hopes for the future of the Chattanooga Writers' Guild.

Kate Landers,
CWG President 2022-2023

"Chattanooga Market Place
Sign in 2015"

photograph by Becky Parker

Spring Contest

The Chattanooga Writers' Guild Spring Writing Contest of 2022 was open to locals of the Chattanooga area, as well as all its members regardless of their location. This was an opportunity to celebrate and support our local writing community. All judging was done in-house, i.e. by our peers. Thank you to everyone who worked hard to make this contest happen - our judges, our promoters, and of course the writers who entrusted us with their prose and poetry. We are delighted to share our 1st, 2nd, and 3rd place winners with you.

"Point Park View"
photograph by Mark Anderson

FICTION

Food for the Soul

by Alexandria Kelly

The night air was thick and humid as Hannah's nerves crawled across her skin like ants. The campus's main art building towered in front of her like a sleeping behemoth with one eye open- a single classroom still lit at this hour. It beckoned her to enter past the poster-covered glass doors with signs advertising everything from roommates to blood drives, and yet she was a statue cemented in the pavement.

She shouldn't be here, in spite of every voice in her head screaming that she should be. The rainbow-colored flier folded in her hoodie pocket felt far too heavy for a single scrap of paper. She traced the words on the page once more, as if this time they would finally stop making her mind rock back and forth like a game of tug-of-war. She lowered her head, as if trying to hide behind her long brown hair and the loose fabric of her oversized hoodie. Why had she ever thought she could do this?

"You lost?"

The mousy girl nearly leapt out of her skin before spinning around to face the source of her shock. Hannah took note of a few things all at once- black hair, brown eyes, dark skin- but the overwhelming sentiment her mind conjured was that this girl was the sort of pretty to bring her internal debate to a frenzy. The word beautiful echoed like a mantra. Hannah's gaze dipped to the bowl the other girl held like an offering, filled to the brim with brightly wrapped chocolates. There was a sticker on her shirt with a name printed in a loose, bubbly script.

Kaylee (She/Her).

"Uh- meeting-" she fumbled out before aborting that entire sentence. "I think I should... leave, actually."

"Promise we don't bite," Kaylee offered with a hopeful smirk.

Hannah chewed her lip as her tennis shoe toed a line in the sidewalk. "It's not exactly the people inside I'm worried about."

She gave an understanding hum. "You from around here?"

"My family lives a few hours away."

"Well, unless they show up, I promise no one will know you were here," she said with a shrug. Her eyes roamed over Hannah for a moment before she sidled the bowl onto her hip and pulled out a pen with a click. "You got something I can write on?"

She blinked owlishly before tugging out the folded-up flier. "This alright?"

Kaylee gave a faint laugh that had no business sounding that sweet as she scribbled out a few digits. "I've got to go, but if you ever wanna chat, text me!" The pen was closed with a click. "I'm Kaylee."

"Hannah," she replied, staring at the flier as if seeing paper for the first time.

"Whatever you decide, take a candy for the road?" The bowl was held out in offering. Without thinking, she snagged an aluminum wrapped chocolate from the array. "Try not to be a stranger," Kaylee called over her shoulder as she walked up the steps. She vanished beyond the array of multicolored posters as Hannah watched.

She clutched at the paper in disbelief. She had made a friend- or potentially more? Her cheeks felt warm and not from the lingering heat in the air. Deciding her heart needed a moment to reign itself in, she unwrapped the simple Hershey's Kiss.

The foil was binned before she popped the dollop of chocolate into her mouth. She let it melt on her tongue even as the tip jabbed at the roof of her mouth. The odd shape of the sweet brought back memories of waving goodbye to her grandparents, even though they had lived not ten minutes down the road. Grandpa had adored Hershey's Kisses and always offered her one as she was heading out the door.

I love you.

She recalled a thousand instances of saying it back- even when he was too ill to leave his bed. The bowl of kisses on his nightstand had been emptied after that and never refilled.

Now, she let the sweetness catch in her teeth as she chewed. She would follow Kaylee as soon as-

A tall, bony figure in the shadows caught her eye. He stood between the campus lampposts, in the dimness where the light was thinnest. She couldn't see his face, but she knew that thin frame. Even from a distance she could make out his long, yellowed nails and the way his hands curled like stiff, broken hinges around his swollen knuckles.

It didn't matter that he couldn't be here. He was, and suddenly all she could recall was the way his nose had crinkled in disgust when her cousin brought his boyfriend to Thanksgiving dinner. He took one slow, shaky step.

Hannah turned and ran as fast as her feet would carry her.

Only behind the locked doors of her dorm room did she stop and try to ease the pounding of her heart.

-

The yellowed restaurant lights gave the seating area a cozy atmosphere. Something twangy played through cheap speakers overhead as Hannah's leg bounced against the red, cushioned seat. Condensation gathered on the side of the transparent plastic cup that she sipped from. The tea was a few notches from being as sweet as soda; in short, perfect. The air condition blew against the back of her neck, now exposed with her far shorter haircut.

It felt like a weight lifted in the most literal sense.

Kaylee leaned forward onto the table between them. "You sure you're alright?"

She gave an apologetic look as she pushed the cup aside. "No, no- I'm... This is good. We've gone out plenty of times together so why would this be a problem?"

A brow quirked. "Because we weren't dating before."

Hannah glanced aside- eyes flicking across the others in the room.

She didn't catch any openly harsh looks, though she chalked it up to their proximity to the campus.

"We can go back to the dorm," Kaylee offered- and it pulled the quiet girl's attention back to her. Her wine-red lips tugged into a smile, but it was one tinged with pity- like she was coaxing a scared animal out of a corner. "Just say the word."

"This is fine," she insisted again. "Promise."

The words had barely left her mouth when their plates arrived. She took in the sight of the fried, golden exterior of a catfish beside a side of string beans and fried okra.

"I didn't know you like okra," Kaylee commented after the waitress left.

Hannah shrugged. "My Grandpa introduced it to me. I don't know... I felt like- something nostalgic?" Maybe it could offset the anxiety stirring in her stomach like a hurricane of hornets.

Her fork jabbed at one of the not-quite-hexagonal pieces before biting into it. The crisp outside broke with a faint crunch, but it was the inside that truly stirred her memories. The texture was tender and slick as the seed pods burst between her teeth. She recall hanging on Grandpa's elbow and as he shared some of his portion with her.

Before she could even ask how Kaylee was enjoying her own meal, she saw a gray uniform shirt materialize over her girlfriend's shoulder. When her eyes dragged up to his face, her heart seized in her chest.

It was like staring at stop lights at night in the rain- as if too many images were overlapping and smearing together all at once, leaving an unknowable, skin-toned blur. She could see a tuft of steel gray hair or the outline of an ear, but trying to comprehend his expression was impossible- if his eyes were even there in the unclear specter's visage.

"Hannah?" Blue eyes snapped back to her girlfriend. Kaylee's brows were knit in concern. She glanced over her shoulder but appeared to see nothing before she turned back to her. "What's wrong?"

Ice was in her veins. Her blue gaze flicked between the gentle eyes of her girlfriend, framed by bright, glittery mascara, to the skin-toned void of what was once her Grandpa. Was that shadow a grimace? Was that smear a glare?

She stood quickly, shame coiling in her gut twofold. She gaped like a gasping fish before pointing in the vague direction of the door. "I'll be right back," she said in a rush before nearly dashing to the exit.

His head followed her even as she hurried away.

She shivered from more than the cold as the night chill brought goosebumps to her arms. After several long moments, she heard the door open before Kaylee joined her beneath the restaurant's awning. "You wanna talk?"

"...I don't know," she whispered. She moved to blot her eyes with her wrist, only to realize the oversized hoodie sleeves weren't there. She had dressed in a floral top that she had felt cute in when she left the dorm. Now, she only wanted to vanish back into that loose, fabric armor.

"If this is too fast-"

"It's not!" she said, meeting her eyes desperately. "I've been looking forward to this all week and I- I want it to be fine because it is. It should be. But I feel like any second someone I know will show up and then my parents will know and- I don't know."

The quiet stretched between them like a chasm, filled only by the distant sound of unintelligible voices inside.

Finally, Kaylee stepped close and put a hand on her arm. "You'll still be you. No matter what ends up happening." She gave a sympathetic smile before letting her hand fall away. "Let's go back inside and at least get some to-go boxes."

"...Alright," she said lowly.

She slunk back into the restaurant, defeat heavy on her shoulders. The ghost was gone, but that did little to ease her mind as they walked back to campus. With each step, however, the quiet girl plucked at the threads of her resolve in an effort to weave them into a plan.

She had a spirit to deal with.

-

It was a quiet Sunday morning in the dorm. The sky was shifting from navy to the pale blue dawn outside her window, though the sun had yet to peek over the horizon in earnest. She plucked a red plastic container from the pantry and set it on the kitchen table, along with a handful of Hershey's Kisses. Hannah preferred her caffeine in the form of energy drinks, but already the scent coming from the tub was stirring at memories of her grandparent's kitchen. The Keurig wasn't the stained white coffee machine she saw in her memories, but it could spit out hot water just the same.

She grabbed a small spoon and took a seat with the steaming mug. The amount of water had mostly been guesswork, but she distinctly recalled how he liked it. She had 'helped' him with it more than once, when she was barely tall enough to see over the countertop. She stared down at her mug as she dumped into two generous spoonfuls of Folgers and stirred.

No sugar. No milk. She could smell the rich bitterness long before she carefully brought it to her lips. It tasted dark and nearly burnt her tongue. She continued to sip at it, even as the man across the table began to materialize.

"...Hi, Grandpa." Her voice was quiet and uncertain, but she forced herself not to look away. His face was still shrouded in an unknowable, skin-hued blur. "I probably look a little different, huh? We both kinda do." She ran a hand through her shorter hair with a sardonic smirk. She took a shaky breath and tried to persist. "...I don't want to keep seeing you like this. I need to live my life without you hovering over my shoulder every time I eat something that reminds me of you."

Grandpa was silent. He didn't even move.

Her grip tightened on the mug that was almost too hot against her fingertips. "Why are you even doing this? You were always kind and patient... at least to most people." She swallowed thickly. "I remember the faces you made whenever there was a gay couple on tv. You never said much, but you nodded along when Uncle Harry said it was an abomination. Like two people being in love was sinful just because-"

Her throat burned as frustrated tears wet her eyes. She brought the mug to her lips and took a long, slow drag of the bitter coffee. Then, she bored her gaze into where his eyes might have been.

"You told me to be kind. So why did yours stop at anyone who wasn't like you? I'm supposed to just- act like that part was something beyond your control? Like you didn't know better?" Now the tears spilled down her cheeks in burning trails. "Do you know how hard it's been to unlearn what you and everyone else taught me? Do you know how long I hated myself because I thought something was wrong with me?!"

There wasn't an answer. He didn't even move. Hannah glared into the dark ripples inside the mug.

"I want to think you would've liked Kaylee, but... I know better. I just-wish you could see her the way I do." Now she lifted her blue eyes. "I wish you could see me the way I do. Because despite it all- I still remember the Grandpa who brushed my hair and bandaged my skinned knees. Who didn't get mad even when I got paint on his favorite tie. But I have to live with the fact that- that you... you probably hate who I am now." The mug was pushed away. She sank down in her chair as she pillowed her head in her arms. The cool table was a balm against her flushed face.

For a time, it was quiet. Then, she heard a soft rustling. When she lifted her head, he was still a ghastly thing to observe- hands skeletal and yet swollen at the joints. His face was unknowable as she watched him push a single aluminum wrapped chocolate across the table.

Hannah longed to see his eyes. Did he look on her like a terminal patient beyond help, or was there a spark of understanding? His obscured face revealed nothing. Grandpa nudged the chocolate closer with a shaking hand.

I love you.

A sob burned in her throat as she picked it up. For a brief moment, her hand brushed through his. She felt only air.

"I love you too," she croaked.

She wiped at her tears before unwrapping the kiss. By the time it had dissolved into nothing in her mouth, Grandpa had faded. Hannah walked over to the kitchen window to watch the sunrise. As the bitter coffee spiraled down the drain, she held her phone to her ear.

"Morning Kaylee. Sorry if I woke you. I was just wondering- do you think we could try that date again?"

From Memory

by Kathy Bowe

The hard leather soles of his polished loafers click and crunch up the walkway. He looks up at the stately brick Colonial and his eyes instinctively focus on the second-floor west bedroom window. But its black reflection only mirrors the tops of the nearby oak tree.

How many days had his eyes traveled to that same spot, to see the pale yellow glow of her table lamp? How his heart would lift at that anemic light!

Some nights the anticipation would be so strong that he would drift off the sidewalk a block from the house, travel down the center of the street, so he could spot that window just a few moments earlier. From that angle, at certain times of year, the sun would guide his gaze straight through the glass to her headboard, to the faint outline of her face against the stack of pillows. He would soften his step, shrink his chin into his collar, whisper his thoughts, as if he were passing a sleeping doe, though in reality she was dozens of yards, two stories, and a double pane away. Don't move, don't startle, just stay exactly there, like that. Please.

But she didn't. The light changed, the reflection disappeared, and not long after that she began coughing blood. Just a little at first, and she tried to hide it in her tissues, buried at the bottom of the waste can. Then more and more. And then she couldn't hide it anymore and bits of lung would follow, her body trying one last-ditch effort to shake the disease. That final day, he drifted to the center of the road and noticed the light was bright, too bright, and he knew. He knew before he reached the walk, before he saw the idling ambulance in the driveway.

He enters the house this day, through the yawning front entrance with its ornate glass side windows that pitch and distort the view of his beagle's happy nose and notes how the silence rings the same as it did when she was upstairs. For so long, he was struck by the stillness of the house every evening despite its constant occupant. She refused a television. She had always insisted they don't belong in the bedroom, even after being bedridden for months. He was fond of TV though, and had never quite adjusted to falling asleep in silence night after night. Still, he had complied with her wishes ever since she moved in with him all those years ago, removing the large and awkward tube-style model from his apartment's bedroom in a show of romanticism that aggravated his hernia.

Years later, she would bring up the television-removal story at parties, smile gently at him, squeeze his arm. When she could no longer attend those parties, could barely squeeze his arm, when pieces of her spattered the tissues, he would search her face for that same soft look of appreciation that made his heart bounce. The look gradually faded as the tissues filled the waste can. He began spending more time downstairs with 42" flat screen, nodding off to Sports Center or CNN until longing, or perhaps guilt, brought him up to the silent room and its increasingly hollow occupant.

This day, brushing past his desperately lonely dog, he leaves the television off. This day, he shuffles out of his loafers as he walks, shrugs out of his coat and lets it crumple to the floor. He walks through the house, making a slow, deliberate round of every room, pausing at this framed print of daisies in a glass, at that pyramid of satin floor pillows, at those bone-shaped dog bowls on elevated steel legs. He has no memories of obtaining any of these items, of delighting at them in stores, of packing the car with them, of peeling their tags, of placing them in their chosen spots in each room. He remembers tripping over the pillows once, and vaguely nodding when a visitor commented on how the colors in the print accented the walls so well. These items speak of and to her, and without her they stand dull and dusty.

He stops at the patio doors and slides them open, allowing his dog a few moments of exuberance in the tidy yard. He watches as the undersized beagle, whom she named Peanut, slides his muzzle deep into the grass, sneezing and groaning. His eyes follow Peanut's jaunt into the dead flower garden, his ears hear the snapping of the dried stems, his skin prickles as he fights back tears. Had it been worse when she was upstairs, coughing out her lung tissue? There were nights when she wept and wheezed for so many hours, when all he could do was stroke her hair and make motherly hushing noises. Those nights, he thought at the time, were the bottom of everything. Watching helplessly as she suffered, sleeping sporadically between fits and sobs, watching another desolate sunrise through the filmy curtains. But now, watching Peanut relieve himself amid the greying moldy stalks of her once-blooming garden, he longs for those nights. How they ended with him stumbling into the shower, drunk with exhaustion, dressing in the half-light, and finally holding her tired face between his tired hands and gently kissing her cold lips. She suffered so much at the end, he thought, but I suffer more now and with no blessed darkness in sight.

He is jarred from his reverie by the doorbell. He stands puzzled, not immediately recognizing the sound. No one comes to the house anymore. The only time that bell rang was for the Tuesday oxygen delivery. He stands still, not responding, watching Peanut tear back into the house to the front hallway, yapping wildly at the distorted face that swims through the side window. They'll go away, he thinks, but as he thinks this he crosses to the door. Go away, he thinks as he opens it a crack, sees the young man in the delivery uniform, holds Peanut back with one stocking foot as he signs for the package. Go away, he thinks, even after the man has gone away.

It's a plain, brown box, the size and shape of a loaf of bread. Blank on every side, sealed with clear cellophane packing tape. One square white label on a top corner, computer-generated machine font. Their address. Only her name. Go away, he thinks.

In the kitchen, he sits at the breakfast counter and slits the tape with a butter knife. Immediately beneath the flap is a flyer for the vendor, an online store where independent artists sell their work. Then, a pile of crinkled brown packing papers. Then, a canvas print carefully wrapped in layers of gauzy sheets of white fabric. Small. The size of a paperback book. Her face, hand painted in whimsical pastels. So thick with paint he sees the bumps of color rising up from the canvas. Her face, recreated from a photo taken the day she had moved into his apartment. Hair pulled up in a messy knot, tipping a beer bottle vaguely at the camera. The bottle was actually brown, but in the painting it's a vibrant cascade of yellows. Her face, glowing in shades of what should be unnatural shades of pink and green but somehow reflecting truth. Her face, smiling up at him. At the bottom of the box, a note from the artist: *Sorry for the delay! I wanted to be sure and get the colors exactly right. I hope you and your husband are pleased with the finished work. Happy Anniversary, and please take a moment to leave me a 5-star review! Sincerely, Anna T.*

He places the artist's note back in the box, then the packing papers, the discarded white cloth. Tucks the flaps down, presses them flat, as if trying to reseal the empty box. Pushes it across the counter. Sets the print in front of him, propping it against her cookie jar shaped like a pig in a chef's hat. Stares at it for how long? Minutes maybe. An hour maybe. Until it felt right to him. Until he knew the bumps and colors well enough. Until he knew he had a job to do.

He had to find the perfect place for this. The perfect room to display this piece, the perfect shelf, the perfect spot on that shelf. A spot among the daisy artwork, the satin pillows, the years filled with her colors. In their home.

Discovery

by Barbara Graham Tucker

Francis Bennett decided to sell off the furniture first. It would take a while and give her time to get past her mother's death before digging deeper into closets and the attic. It would allow her to keep up the utilities and insurance and postpone the sale of the house a little longer. Yes, she was only delaying the inevitable. Her mother's house, the home where they had spent so many family events, would have to go into other hands. Either a young family who could raise their children, or an investor who would turn it into an AirBnB like so many were doing in this part of town.

Throughout the fall, the house grew increasingly emptier. In fact, as the larger items left, thanks mostly to CraigList and Facebook Market, the house seemed bigger than when it was full of chairs and couches and beds and tables. Now, the big furniture, none of it high end, but all of it sturdy and functional, was gone from 611 Forrester Avenue.

On this October Saturday, when so much of the region was either cheering a college team or attending a school festival, she unlocked the door to 611 Forrester and let herself into the mostly bare 1960's rancher.

It was her mother's second home. Mavis Townsend, a widow with three grown children, relocated at 65. Her mother bought it on her own after depending on Dad for 45 years. She bought it to live near Frances twenty years ago, making her own decisions, sort of, after letting her husband make them for so long. Mom had not downsized, not much, when she sold the home Frances grew up in and moved here. And in two decades, she had accumulated almost as much as in those 45 years of her adult, married life.

Frances set her purse down. She had to think this through, which closet to attack first. She could just jump in, but she didn't even know what was in some of those closets. And she was hungry. Frances decided to eat her scone and drink the latte first.

She eased into the camping chair she kept there for sitting, now that all the furniture was sold. Last week, she also brought in a folding table for sorting whatever came out of the closets and attic. That, and scissors, packing tape, and twenty-seven good sized, double-enforced boxes from Home Depot should get her through the day.

She sipped coffee and nibbled the scone, thinking at the same time there was too much sugar in both and she was courting A1C and glucose trouble with every bite and gulp. She surveyed the house. Whoever ended up buying it had their work cut out for them. Structurally sound, but woefully out of date. Shag carpet in most of the rooms—orange in some, no less. Well, not quite orange, maybe, but garish nonetheless. Mom had so wanted to get new carpet and drapes. But her Social Security from Dad just didn't extend that far. Mom had been a homemaker all her life, pure and simple, a rarity now.

Yet it was a place of happy memories. Frances' brothers' families came here for the holidays, a long trip from their homes in Dayton. But Frances figured she was the daughter, she'd be the one expected to take care of Mom in the waning years, and it made more sense for Mom to be near her.

Frances saw children running through the rooms. Her brothers and husband watching football in the "den," as Mom called it. Mom cooking those dishes she perfected—nothing fancy, but delicious and comforting. Mom's swollen ankles and crooked fingers didn't keep her from cooking the Thanksgiving turkey and stuffing it with bread crumb dressing. Living in this southern city, Frances had adapted the "dressing" alternative; the thought of something baked in the turkey turned her stomach a bit now, even though she'd been raised on it. Sort of like liver; organ meats made her gag.

Frances wiped her hands and mouth from the last of the too-rich coffee and too-sweet scone, stood up, stretched, pulled the folding table into the hallway near the linen closet, and began to dig.

The linen closet was true to form. Lots of towels and sheets, most warn to the point of uselessness. Some sheets almost see-through thin, towels and washcloths with hem long ragged and torn. A few might help—who? Really? No, except for about five of the intact towels, which she would take, the rest were discards.

The bottom of the closet yielded on old glass humidifier—really old; surely they used it as children in the 1960s? Another discard; the cord was frayed and the plug not a "three-pronger" anyway. Why had Mom kept such a thing? Frances found boxes of cleaning rags and old bottles of Mr. Clean, dust polish, and such. Trash, trash, trash.

That closet done, she moved to the first bedroom closet, the room reserved for visiting grandchildren to sleep in. Frances dubbed this the Christmas stuff closet. Oh, my word. She'd have to find that card from the flea market woman who saw her ads on Craigslist. Unless Frances was willing to have a yard sale—and she wasn't—this stuff just needed "to go to a good home," as they said. In this case, they would end up at that woman's stall in the loosely named "antique mall" out by the Interstate.

Mom loved Christmas. Frances had trouble getting a tree up. Too much other work to do. Jenny and Philip's music programs. Social commitments. Church events. Shopping. Parties at the office. That was the difference; Mom had always been a housewife in that way of her generation. Frances made a home a differently, especially after Richard left the children and her and disappeared for six months. He landed in a mental health facility in Florida after being arrested for causing a disturbance in a public library and arrested. That led to five years of chaos and a brutal divorce that no one understood, she didn't want, and served no purpose in helping Richard. It only kept her from being legally responsible for him. Christmas decorations faded in importance for Frances and stayed that way.

Anyway, Mom's Christmas items were old, dusty, and of little value to anyone. But there sure were enough of them. Good grief. Yes, she'd have to call that woman. Maybe she could come get them later today. Frances didn't frequent flea markets and antique malls unless she was on a mission. And Frances was usually on a distinct mission.

That closet emptied and the items put by the garage door, Frances moved to her mother's better guestroom. This closet held Mom's winter clothes. She pushed those aside, knowing all but a few of the them would go in the garbage. Frances read on the Internet that the clothes Americans think go to charity, don't always. Charities couldn't keep up with flood of old clothes. She could donate to the church closet, some coats, maybe. Otherwise, these items were destined for big black plastic bags and the landfill.

Behind the clothes, however, Frances found something that made her stop. In fact, it made her stop breathing for a few seconds. Some might call it a fairy tale treasure trove. Gold and silver boxes, *glittery* gold and silver, at least originally. These were old packages. Old gifts, decades old, from the faded look of the paper and ribbons. Or at least some of them; definitely they varied in age.

What in the world? Frances said out loud. This was unexpected. She'd never seen these boxes—how had she missed them in 58 years of being Mavis' daughter? What were they? They looked like wedding gifts, of all things

Frances sighed. She really wanted to stay on pace and finish cleaning out the house today. These boxes were not part of the plan. There were dozens of them. She would have to go through them slowly, and carefully. It would take at least an hour.

She decided to finish scouring the rest of the house and come back to them at the end.

The packages waited as they had for, probably, over half a century. The packages whispered to Frances as she dug and tossed and pulled and dumped. Why would her mother have dozens of apparently unopened gift boxes hidden in the back of a closet? Hidden? Yes, definitely hidden. What secrets were there? What else would she find?

Damn. This is so niggling. Focus, Frances. Get this done.

At 1:00 she packed the back of her Nissan Rogue for a trip to the landfill and to visit a drive-through for a sandwich. She made it just before the landfill closed.

Exhausted, she let herself back into Mom's house. She would call her real estate agent, after cleaning was done, a semi-friend of a semi-friend, to put it on the market. The sooner the better. Mom was gone, and the house was now only a burden. It only had meaning when Mom lived here and loved here, sat in her favorite chair and watched her grandchildren and later, great grandchildren play with their Christmas presents, compete in Uno tournaments, and get away with naughtiness because she was the grandma.

Frances pulled the camping chair into the guestroom and planted it by the closet. She re-opened the closet and reached for the first box on the first stack. Its size led her to expect it to weigh four or five pounds. Instead, it was weightless.

It felt empty. She shook it. No sound but the faint rustle of the stiff ribbon. Frances inspected it. It was carefully wrapped, with sharply folded paper and evenly distributed clear tape. It showed no signs of having ever been unwrapped. She laid it on floor gingerly, even though she was sure it was empty.

She reached for the one that had been under it; larger and just as weightless. Then the ones below that, of equal size. Then the next stack. And the next. Most were basically rectangular, but some were six by six inches, some flatter, some tall and slender. All diligently wrapped. All seemingly empty.

She had moved all the packages from the closet to the barren bedroom's floor. She sat in the camping chair, surrounded by them. What was this about? What had her mother been doing? For how long? Was it a dementia thing? No. At the beginning, before she touched the first one, she thought they might be unopened, or unused wedding gifts. But over lunch she knew that couldn't be right. Mom and Dad had married when he got back from Korea, in a small courthouse wedding with a few friends followed by dinner out and a three-day honeymoon to Niagara Falls, of course, where couples up north went. Frances had seen the photos, the simple black and whites of her mom in a light linen suit and huge corsage and her dad in a sharp pinstripe suit. No tulle and tuxedo, just simple, how most people did it in the early '50s. This number of wrapped gifts would have meant sixty or eighty guests. Mom was frugal but liked her nice things; she would have found a way to use gifts.

Even stranger, the further back into the closet she reached, the dustier and more faded the packages became. By the time she pulled the last one out, its paper tore at her touch.

She knew they couldn't be truly empty. She placed the oldest one in her lap and tried to open it without tearing it more, but that was impossible. The paper disintegrated, so she ripped it off. She lifted the lid. Inside she found a slip of paper.

She slapped the lid back on the box. She felt her skin redden and heat up. She knew, in a flash of emotion and insight, that to read that slip would take her into a world she didn't want to enter. Her mother's internal world. Whatever was written on that slip of paper, and she could only conclude that every other box had another slip, with a different message, probably, was something her mother wanted hidden. Not "something." Many things, hidden from everyone and yet kept near her, for years, for whatever reasons. Clearly these boxes didn't represent dementia symptoms. The only dementia might have come from Mom not getting rid of them before she died.

Mom's death at 86 was from a combination of congestive heart failure and hemorrhagic stroke. The stroke led to a fall, a broken hip, and Mom's inability to push her Life Guard button, so she lay there too long before she was found and the stroke's effects were irreversible. After a few days in the hospital, Mom died. No months of lingering from cancer. No years of decline from Alzheimer's, no long stays in a nursing facility with a memory care center, where Frances would have to visit and wrangle with staff and Medicare and all that. Quick, sudden, final, with no time to make amends or destroy the packages or give directions. One of her friends had the nerve to tell Frances this was the best way to lose her mother, one of those careless, mindless things people lovingly say to the grieving.

Perhaps Mom planned to tear them all apart, burn them, put them in big black garbage sacks and set them out by the curb, a last act of penance or forgiveness or absolution, all those religious words out of place in their family and upbringing. Well, Frances would never know about that. She did know she must either open each package and read each slip, consume each message, absorb each thought or sin or pain. Or. She must build a fire in the back yard and burn them all to ashes within the half hour.

The choice came down to two arguments. Either Mom wanted them found and wanted Frances to read them. Or reading them would be a great violation.

No, what really mattered was whether Frances could bear to read them, to know her mother's real heart, to know what pained and drove and disappointed Mavis Townsend for 65 or more years, through marriage and three children, moving and starting a new life in her senior years, seven grandchildren, losing a husband, living on Social Security, facing age and infirmity, death, wanting, not having, loving, losing. To know the truth of it all.

***

At four o'clock Frances locked the front door. She'd have to leave the bags and packed and sealed brown boxes in the back of the SUV until she could get to the landfill later that week. She could smell the cinders and fumes on her clothes, and was glad Mom's neighbors had not asked her what she was burning or complained about the smoke.

"Cannon on Lookout Mountain"
photograph by Adam L. Massey

CREATIVE NONFICTION

Experiencing Grace in the Year 2020

by Sherry Poff

I sit in the bright school lobby at ten o'clock of an autumn morning. Sun shines through large front windows and creates a criss-cross of shadows on the gray-washed wood floor. My creative writing students sit nearby, observing and making notes. A shuffle of footsteps gets our attention as the music teacher comes through with kindergarten students in a wiggly line. They stop by the welcome desk to wait for their classroom teacher. Mrs. Ferrel walks down the line squirting hand sanitizer into their open palms.

"I have some people who are not listening," she says. "Clayton, come get in line. . . . Clayton, I'm waiting for you. Clayton . . . ." The kindergarteners whisper and squirm, beckoning to their errant classmate.

"Now rub your hands together." Mrs. Ferrel demonstrates, intertwining her own fingers and moving her hands briskly.

The front door buzzes, and Renee, the receptionist, cranes her neck to see who's outside before pushing the unlock button. It's a senior boy, mumbling excuses for signing in late. The assistant principal breezes through, surveys the scene, waves to everyone, and keeps moving.

A gray phone on the desk chimes and chimes again. Renee reaches for the receiver. "Good morning. Grace Academy!"

Grace is an apt name for our small private school in East Tennessee. And grace is what the community is experiencing. For a while, though, life was hard. Most of the school's seventeen buildings were destroyed in a tornado on Easter night, 2020. Rain and wind rearranged not just our structures but our lives. Already home to avoid spreading COVID-19, we hardly had time to adjust to one change before another one came charging at us.

In the week after the storm, teachers were allowed to visit our storm-ravaged classrooms and retrieve what we could. We showed up in masks, bearing boxes and Rubbermaid containers, reaching out for tentative hugs. We carried away folders, desk supplies, miscellaneous books dotted with water drops and insulation fibers, and never-to-be-forgotten images of our ruined spaces. The containers we stowed in basements, extra bedrooms, empty corners, under tables and behind beds. We filled our cars' trunks and borrowed space from relatives until we might have our own buildings again. The memories haunt us still.

All that spring I sat in a kitchen chair at a round table near my front window, the light on my face through open blinds as I interacted with my students online, searching their digital faces for signs of despair or hope, drawing their attention to *Julius Caesar* and urging them to finish up research papers. It became harder and harder to pull them from their warm beds, extract a reaction to Thomas Hardy, focus attention on new vocabulary. Days grew longer and warmer as the forsythia faded and azaleas and dogwoods opened up. School hours blended imperceptibly with after-school. Evenings seemingly created for baseball were spent in solitary strolls around the neighborhood, waving to friends from the middle of the street or passing discreetly on the other side. No spring soccer, no softball tournaments, and no prom. The day set aside for this annual rite of passage was fabulously warm and bright. I couldn't help mourning the pictures that would never be taken, memories lost before they could be formed.

Driving past our damaged campus became more and more discouraging as greening vegetation highlighted missing treetops and distorted branches. The school staff gathered on a warm Sunday afternoon for a final picture with the old buildings before demolition began. Though we were happy to see colleagues, the mood was strained, and we eventually drifted apart to gaze across the rubble at broken cabinets, water-logged tables, and jumbled band instruments just out of reach. The future, always a mystery, seemed particularly uncertain.

Within weeks of our photography session, we got word from our Head of School that a large church in the area had offered the use of their facilities for as long as we needed. School officials spent the summer working out the details: assigning classrooms, assessing space, installing wifi, and arranging orientation sessions with small groups of staff members to avoid spreading the virus. And now here we are in our temporary home.

The door buzzes again, and Renee reaches to release the lock. "Dad of the year, comin' your way!" she calls. "It's good to see you again---and again." She and RJ's dad both laugh as he sets a blue backpack on the counter. "I'll see that he gets this," Renee promises.

It's almost time for the next class, so I signal for my students to wrap up their work. As I wait for them, I survey a table near the door stacked with literature books, iPads, and math texts for pickup. In a few hours, a dad, a grandmother, or a kind neighbor will stop by to retrieve these items and deliver them to Grace students who are choosing to continue distance learning a little longer. I nod hello to another staff member. Deborah is here to help with extra cleaning during the pandemic. We don't know enough about the virus to understand all the possible dangers, but we are doing everything we can to be safe and to make sure we can keep meeting our students in person.

It takes a lot of cooperation to keep a school running in ordinary times, but this year is stretching us in unusual ways. A swirling wind laid bare the artifacts of our personal and professional lives, and a storm of troubles uncovered details of our national life that have required special attention as well. A sign in the main lobby bears the motto of the church that meets here: Love, Learn, Live. I like to think--I dare to hope-- that all across the country, not only here in our piece of the Tennessee valley, we are learning to love and to live better than ever before.

Bittersweet Reckoning: A Real Mother's Day

by Amy White Ziegler

I need to make peace with Mother's Day. As a mother now, I'm supposed to enjoy it. But rarely have I found the day enjoyable. Every year in May, TV commercials present strange visions of what celebrations of mom should look like. Ornate outdoor brunches under a flowered trellis. Flowing dresses and weird hats. Husbands presenting diamond necklaces and bracelets because their wife is a 24-year-old model. Children in unwrinkled pajamas bringing breakfast to a smiling, awake mother as she reclines in bed. This isn't what Mother's Day is like . . . or what the day brings to mind for so many of us.

One of my friends tried to warn me. She had gotten married and had three children while I was still single and lingering in graduate school. After I wished her "Happy Mother's Day" one year, she said it wasn't her favorite holiday. In fact, she secretly wished the day didn't exist. I was shocked. Why would any mother say that? She explained that the day can't live up to media hype or the way mothers are idealized, put on pedestals. The reality of actual life with actual children during the 24 hours called "Mother's Day" never lives up to that ideal vision. Toddlers find a way of acting horrible on that Sunday, she said. They realize the day isn't about them and can be absolute stinkers, refusing to celebrate properly or pose for pictures. Husbands can't read your mind and need to be told what gift to get you. According to her, the whole ordeal would be better if it weren't such a big deal, or any deal at all. I told her I was sorry, that I would never tell her "Happy Mother's Day" again. I wondered, could it be that bad?

Years later, I understood exactly what my friend was talking about. When my daughter was ages 1, 2, and 3, I realized that I needed to do the same amount of work to keep her fed and alive on that special day as I did on every other day of the year. Yes, her father shares the parenting load and helps a lot. But the list of things only Mommy does right still exists every Mother's Day. The mental checklist also exists—that set of unwritten agenda items that need to be checked off for the family to function properly. Mothers can't call in a substitute teacher because it's a holiday.

As my daughter grew slightly older, she wanted every day to be about her. Mother's Day directly thwarted her central desire. One year, in her five-year-old self-centeredness, she refused to stand next to me for a Mother's Day picture. When we finally bribe-forced her to do so, it was incredibly hard to get her to make one decent smile for one decent picture. I realized that she probably had a subconscious impulse to mess up her mom's special day. I told myself, she's just a kid being a kid; don't take it personally. But I was mad at my child for acting so childish. This was what my friend had warned me about. The reality of Mother's Day never matches the promise shown in Hallmark or Kay Jewelry commercials. Kids don't want society or their dads to tell them on which day they're supposed to display perfect behavior. On that Sunday, mothers of children still have to raise their voice or resort to the usual threats. It's a day like any other.

As a mom, I see plenty of disappointment baked into this holiday. Yet even before becoming a mom, my history with the second Sunday in May was difficult.

Mother's Day is painful for women who want to be mothers, but aren't. When I was still single, in my late 20s and early 30s, I hated Mother's Day because it reminded me that I was at least two major life stages away from being a mom. I wasn't even married. I sat through many church services that seemed to affirm that motherhood was the best possible state a woman could achieve. I remember walking into my grandparents' church one year on Mother's Day—a small Pentecostal church in Virginia's Appalachian Mountains—and the pastor's wife started to hand me the pink carnation that all the moms were getting. Then she realized who I was and said, "Oh— you're not a mother." She paused sadly, then said, "Well, here, you can have one anyway." To her credit, this woman was trying to include me in the tribe of honored females. But the message I got was that I had been given a pity flower because I had not become who someone my age should have been by that time—a mother. I had to keep that flower with me throughout the service. The pastor said nothing that morning about women who might have felt sad that day, who wanted to be mothers but weren't. I felt invisible, and also like an imposter who shouldn't be holding a flower. I hated this holiday that forcibly separated women into the The Honored with children and The Unblessed, without children, as if in a scene from *The Handmaid's Tale*.

The pain of my single years, however, was nothing compared to the pain of Mother's Day after I was married and my husband and I struggled to have a baby. I remember changing the channel each time a Mother's Day-related commercial appeared on TV. Nope, not watching that. I was aware every day of the year that I wanted to have a child, so I did not need an extra televised reminder that motherhood is wonderful. Two grandmothers that I adored and my own mother had shown me that already. I considered skipping church that Sunday. But in my sadness, I felt like I deserved to be there just as much as all the moms. During the service, I concentrated on features of sanctuary ceiling lights so that I didn't cry too hard. Dabbing one's face with one Kleenex, silently, is acceptable. Sobbing loudly is not. At least in our large, Washington, D.C.-area church, the pastor prayed for women who wanted to be mothers but weren't. That was only one phrase in a long service, but that moment was meaningful to me. My pain was seen. My reality was on the map of women's experience.

After that Sunday, I thought the holiday couldn't get any worse. One year later, it was. My first miscarriage occurred three days before Mother's Day 2012. Attending a Mother's Day service right after having a miscarriage was a nightmare. I had no other, living children and no guarantee that I ever would have one. The day intended to honor mothers became, for me, the day that put my deepest theological doubts and questions into sharp relief. Why does God allow so many would-be mothers to remain childless? No satisfactory answer exists. The holiday that year was one of the worst days I have ever lived through. I was moving underwater, trying not to choke or drown. I had to make myself eat, but I barely felt like any *self* was there. I had bled away with my child I never met. The grief was unbearable, but carrying that grief on a day called "Mother's Day" felt like the most cruel cosmic joke. It physically hurt to keep breathing.

Two years later, the contrast couldn't have been more dramatic. I was holding my newborn daughter. She had arrived in April 2014 and was a tiny ball of colic that second Sunday of May. I was overjoyed. When I see pictures from that day, I know I'm seeing perhaps the happiest Mother's Day I will ever have. My tired smile is just a hint of what the past few years had required from me. Just as there had been no words to adequately describe my grief two years before, now there were no words for my deep joy. I finally had stepped into the reality of "motherhood" and couldn't believe that my life situation qualified for "Mother's Day." I was in love with my new daughter and thrilled with my new title.

Since 2014, and despite my daughter's misbehavior on certain Mother's Days, I have enjoyed the nice side of this holiday. As a preschooler, my daughter brought home a piece of white cloth covered in random stamps of pink paint. Her beaming face indicated that the only purpose of this cloth was for me to like it, and I did. In kindergarten, she made me a card with a sweet penciled message in shaky capital letters. In first grade, she drew a colorful castle and proclaimed "Happy Mother's Day!" in alternating rainbow colors. Drawing castles was her love language. These are the pieces of Mother's Day I will keep with my best mom artifacts.

Yet no one told me that Mother's Day will always bring to mind all three of my pregnancies: the one that led to my daughter, and the other two, which led to miscarriages. Every May, I am deeply aware that I was almost a mother of three. I lament the two embryos that didn't grow into viable babies. One had developed a heartbeat; the other had not. One was removed all at once in the hospital; we received a genetic analysis and learned what trisomy 13 meant. The other occurred slowly, at home, during a horrible two weeks of hemorrhage. The only thing we learned was that my doctor failed to see the torture of this "natural miscarriage" method. Both embryos were wanted and loved from the first moment I saw the pregnancy test. Both are mourned every May.

Mother's Day is a memorial day for millions of women who have lost pregnancies. If we are fortunate enough to have a living child, or children, the day becomes a bittersweet reckoning of what God has given, and what God has taken away. We are happy to be celebrated for our work on behalf of our children and families. It is nice to be recognized. But no one recognizes the invisible children we may see walking around the house. They are real to us—particularly on Mother's Day. Many of us are grieving—for children we may never have, for children we lost, and for this complex piece of our identity that greeting cards and TV commercials cannot possibly address. Mother's Day is complicated. The day should not be presented in pretty pink flatness with only flowers and diamonds.

Perhaps young women could be told the truth about Mother's Day: it may affect you, even if you're not a mother. For young mothers, it may be a day of disappointment. It may be hard beyond belief. You will probably like whatever cards or flowers you receive. You may or may not like the gifts, though you will appreciate the sentiment of the one who gives them. You may enjoy a nice meal at a restaurant. You may even wear a nice dress or a hat, or eat outside under a flowered trellis. The good parts will be good. But the holiday has a dark side. You may get tired of smiling when you actually feel sad. You may find yourself quietly crying in a closet when it is time to go to brunch. The truth is that how you feel about this day may change, drastically, from year to year.

While I once wished Mother's Day could be canceled, I don't anymore. I want my child to appreciate me each year, just as I want her to appreciate her father each June. I want to appreciate my mom, my mother-in-law, and the grandmothers I miss dearly. Most surprisingly—at least, to myself—I also see the need for one day each year to remind me of pregnancies I've lost. I want to remember the potential of those children and the love I still feel for them. For a few short weeks, I was their mother, too. On at least one day each year, I meditate on being a mother of three.

My Walden

by Mark Anderson

Wyoming is a vast, amazing state, but my summer home was in a small corner of the state, one hundred acres – not my own – but I tended it. For ten years I was camp director, carpenter, janitor, and sometimes the cook. It was a camp on the Bear River, at eight thousand feet, below mountain peaks of twelve thousand feet, in the foothills of the Uinta Mountains, a range shared between Utah and Wyoming. This was my Walden.

I arrive early each spring with snow melting, creeks running high and gray trees with bright green buds. One year, a typical year, upon arriving to camp, walking in a meadow behind the cabins, I encountered a large black moose with her calf, maybe a few hours old. They were near the stream, about fifty yards away, in soft green grass, so I kept my distance and gazed, savoring the precious moment. If I was a threat she could be on me and trample me dead in five seconds. They moved on, with mama nudges and wobbly legs. I wondered; *how many people are blessed with such a rare moment?*

In the cabin I built, but did not own, with the brook by my window, I slept content, like a baby, better than I ever did in the city. Standing outside at night, the stars, set in deep blackness, were magic to my eyes. I found the Big Dipper and the North Star, and listened for night critters.

I awoke in the morning like every human should – to the sound of birds. Standing in a field of wet sage in the morning, the fragrance was intoxicating. In the East they have the fragrance of sycamores and sassafras, but in the West we have sage. Walking to the camp kitchen I would greet all nature as it awakened; ground squirrels coming to the surface and cautiously standing upright, sniffing, their eyes no good. I sat on the kitchen porch with coffee and toast, watching deer grazing across the hillside. All was so peacefully silent, which is hard for a busy minded human to adjust to. All I heard for days was the backdrop of silence, punctuated with the sound of the animals. Two noisy cranes might announce their landing, then silently graze and alternate turns eating and watching for predators. The ground squirrels making calls to their neighbors and starting the day of play. I heard the songs of many small birds and the tapping of a woodpecker in the distance. Later, the scream of my chain saw would disturb all of this.

And then the humans arrived – campers! They came from the city for a short break. They sang, they ran, they played in the river, they sat by the fire, they watched the deer on the hillside, and they wished that they could stay all summer. Mostly they were church groups. One special group was from a homeless shelter. They sat by the fire smoking and talking about recovery. They played horse shoes for hours, then ventured off on a group hike – sober – but intoxicated at being free.

There was one incident with a group of church teens that was exceptional. We were preparing for an evening game, kind of like capture the flag in the dark. At dusk a large bull moose drifted into the meadow where the game was to be played and stood their grazing on willows. Because moose are dangerous we all screamed at it to leave, but it stayed. It just would not be intimidated. We surrendered and decided to have our s'mores first and then go out to play after the moose was gone. So all the campers came to the fire ring, got their marshmallows roasting and started singing. In a few minutes that huge bull moose with its grand antler spread and gray whiskers came around to our fire, stood about twenty feet away, and started grazing while watching us. We screamed in terror for it to leave, but that big old animal just stood there like it was totally curious about us. We chose to embrace the moment and resumed our fun. This was a beautiful close encounter that was so rare that it was almost unbelievable. It was part of the magic of living so close to nature.

One day a group of four deer was crossing the hillside and one dropped out. She stayed around for a month or so; loved to sleep in the shade of the bathhouse. She had sores on her neck making her easy to recognize. I once saw a coyote trying to bite her (they pass the mange disease) she turned upon it and chased it off. She hung around like she was curious about humans. While working I saw her watching me from just thirty feet away. Just laying there in the sage watching. She was so cute that I wanted her to stay as a camp pet, but one day she moved on.

At dusk as I returned to my cabin, I noticed upon the ridge an unusual shape. I looked close for a long time, at first no movement, but then, as they moved I saw two animals. *Were they dogs or coyotes? No, they were fox.* From the ridge crest they could view the meadow below and small critters in the brush. I watched them and they watched me. They began jumping around, playing like puppies. I watched them play until it was dark and time for bed. The next morning as I arose and headed to the kitchen, I was so amazed to see my two friends still there. It was just unbelievable, and made no sense to this human at all. After I greeted them with a hearty good morning they disappeared and I never saw them again.

I was in a clearing in an aspen forest, cutting a log for a project in camp. The sky was brilliant Wyoming blue. At 8,000' elevation the sky is always brilliant. The leaves were rustling in the slight breeze, birds chirping, and a moose was grazing nearby. It was all so peaceful that I could hardly contain myself. I stopped and thought, *this is how humans lived for all human history until the industrial age. People just walked everywhere, in silence and solitude. They sang a song as they walked, or talked out loud, or prayed. Everything was slower, and more connected to nature. I whispered, Thank you God, this is really my niche.*

Now the first snow has fallen, the river runs low and very cold. Beaver are busy, the squirrels are asleep, and the elk bugle nearby. Leaves are falling, the grass has turned white, shadows are long in the afternoon and temperatures drop quickly. Fall has arrived and I prepare the camp for winter closing; clean the kitchen, drain all water lines, and lock the doors for the last time, leaving this precious place to be buried in eight months of snow and cold, waiting in hope of spring.

"Eternal Flame Red Clay"
photograph by Ray Zimmerman

POETRY

There Were Mudskippers in the Creek

by John DeVore

There were mudskippers in the creek
Behind the bearded man's house.
He planted the woods
and built the pine needle covered pathways
that twisted through the half acre space
Behind a modest ranch style dwelling,
Set back a ways from the road,
Bookended by dense and overgrown scrub on either side.

How we found it, I don't remember.
Our lives were lived on other people's land
Sneaking in and out by unworn pathways,
Through briar and bush, over vine and down steep hillsides,
Into gulches that seemed like valleys,
Always following the water that marked the borders of our neighborhood.
We traced it over rocks and small drops into the shallow TVA drained
pools of the Clinch,
Where we crossed sticky river bottoms that often stole our shoes.

We took the black dog with us sometimes.
Her fur was corded in spots, tail curved like a saber
One ice blue eye, the other half brown.
She ran ahead, only circling back if she heard
A cry or a laugh or an insult
She was afraid of men but not of boys or the cows that lived
In the pasture beyond the barbed wire fence by the creek
Where crawdads hid between the rocks.

We crossed that pasture too and found
A deep blue spring that bubbled in the middle
And rusted grey pipes that led far underground.
Above was a dark canopy of shade trees and
We didn't stay long, for the trek home took time
And there was evening church and I had to make sure
To clean the mud from my shoes.

I never knew the bearded man's name,
Even though he talked to us from time to time
And told us about the mudskippers,
And about how he planted the woods
and built the pine needle covered pathways
That twisted through the half acre space
Behind a modest ranch style dwelling,
Bookended by dense and overgrown scrub on either side.

He must have been the one who placed the No Trespassing signs
On the trees by the road where we always entered the woods.
I haven't seen a mudskipper since.

Rock Star Wishes

by Patricia Hope

Stars are really rocks,
ancient, hydrogen
and helium burning
from their core,
shooting points of light
across the universe
millions of miles to
where you and I stand
in the cool night air,
holding hands, our love
hotter than the star's fire,
so sure of each other,
we're willing to hang
our dreams on a rock
the size of a firefly.

Colors of War

by Patricia Hope

I am a soldier. Yesterday, I was a
merchant happy to run my store
and sell my wares to my neighbors.
Today, I weld barriers to hold back tanks,
make Molotov cocktails, and learn how
to load and fire an AK-47.

> Color me grim gray.

I am a boy, just 12 years old, making
my way across the country hundreds
of miles to go to a place I've never been.
I travel alone, dependent on those I meet
for food and shelter. My parents stayed to fight.

> Color me hopeful purple.

I am a pregnant mom. My labor has been
brought on by the bombing of the hospital
where I was admitted earlier today. As I am
hurried across the parking lot to a waiting
rescue vehicle, I realize my baby may never
be born, or if it is, I may not live long enough
to hold him in my arms.

> Color me saddest blue.

I am a Polish woman with empathy
for my neighbors having to flee their home.
But for the grace of God, things could be reversed.
I must help however I can, give them comfort,

food, shelter, clothing, whatever is asked of me.

Color me worried green,

I am an elderly woman who wanted
to spend the rest of my life in peace
in my own home with my family nearby.
I never thought I'd be traveling the refugee
road in 2022. But war has no compassion
for age or gender, no allowance for who
might be homeless or how one might suffer.

Color me faded brown.

I am the enemy. I, too, have family and loved ones
waiting for me at home. I serve my country with
loyalty, even when I am not sure what we are doing
is the right thing to do. I only know how to obey.
I cannot think for myself. That is never allowed
where I come from.

Color me bomb's-red-glare

I am an injured citizen lying beneath the rubble
of my bombed-out apartment building. I pray
that help will come in time, but, if I die, please
don't let it be for nothing. Let the generations
to come know my life counted for freedom.

Color me independent blue
and defiant yellow,
the colors of my flag.

"Chattanooga National Cemetery"
photograph by John C. Mannone

2022 Monthly Contest Series

Our second Monthly Contest series ran from January through October of 2022. We decided to focus our theme for each month on our city and its landmarks, history, and culture, while inviting writers to challenge themselves by writing outside their preferred genre. To enter one month, a short-storyist might have had to write a poem, and the next month a narrative poet might be limited to a haiku. We also decided to try something new - instead of seeking judges each month, the winners were decided by popular vote, open to the public. We enjoyed reading through all the finalists and we are proud to share the winners once more with you here.

January

A journey just begun, or nearing its end

A Fresh Beginning

by Sherry Poff

I broke down and cried when I read that my baby would begin to walk at around a year. I was still amazed by her tiny, perfect ears, hands, and feet. To think of those feet carrying her away from me was more than my postpartum emotions could handle.

Later, my mother held those little pink feet in her own warm hands and remarked, "Where will these little feet go?" Mom was possibly imagining great things for her granddaughter, but I again felt the stab of fear. Was it because my own youthful waywardness was still fresh on my mind? Because I understood with poignant ruefulness that a parent's love and guidance can go only so far? Then we're on our own.

But we're not. We're not on our own. We are created with a yearning for community, and from our first moments of life, we reach for another, we trust another. Children are born with no knowledge of what there is to fear. In most cases, each person they come in contact with in those first weeks and months is a person who wants to help them, someone who loves them and wishes them well. Their first stumbles and scraped elbows help them understand that the world can be a dangerous place. But the ones who come alongside and help them up are part of the learning process as well. Day by day, children learn to take one step and then another, and before we know it, they move with confidence. They become leaders and helpers themselves.

Poet Susan Coolidge noted, "Every day is a fresh beginning." Some like to think of each new year as a fresh beginning. We buy calendars with beautiful, hope-filled images or with funny, hope-inducing messages. We remember that we are not alone, and—perhaps—we resolve to be the one to pick up another.

Everything feels so uncertain just now. But life has always been a tenuous venture. These days we have more resources than ever before, more ways to reach out. We just need to learn—or perhaps remember—how to do that.

February

Love of a Little Debbie

For the Love of a Little Debbie

by Laura Miller

Blue gingham girl,

cake goddess for whom

grown men would battle.

March

The Railroad

The Next Stop

by Daniel Rosas

Markus Nilsson hated traveling. Whether by train or airplane it always started the same. His mum would frantically race about while his dad grumbled and his two siblings would wait 'till the last minute to do anything.

Markus thought it odd that they needed to pack anything just for a trip to the train station. Maybe it was one of those, "spur of the moment trips". Everyone would pile into the car, pick a destination and take-off. Like the time they tramped to an island off the coast of South Carolina that looked like they were the first people to ever have set foot on it. Adventures, his mum would call it.

The trip to the train station was short and Markus gleefully leapt from the car's cramped confines. He grabbed his backpack and started towards the station. In the lobby a woman was seated by a side wall in front of a large black boxy machine. It had a series of white lines cutting across it with buttons and switches at specific points. She was talking into a headset and reached up a few times to push buttons causing lights to turn red, green or white.

Odd, he thought. No trains had run at this station in years. Markus chalked it up to the woman just having fun.

The family entered the lobby under glistening crystalline chandeliers and a stunning high domed ceiling. A circular glass window was set in the middle with a pattern that reminded Markus of a sunflower with rays of bronze light shooting out. They continued out onto a concourse where to the right was a shiny red and green steam locomotive. Chattanooga Choo Choo was written in gold letters on its side. They walked to the passenger platform then past several coaches before his mother stopped and motioned them inside.

Down a narrow corridor were doors on either side. His brother opened a door to his right and his sister took one to the left. Markus went to go with his brother.

"Get your own dork," his brother said.

"Take the next one," his mother instructed with a hint of exasperation.

Markus entered the next cabin. Light poured in through the open drapes. To his right was a long blue seat. Ahead a writing table. To his left was a sink with a mirror.

Markus set his backpack down and went to the window. Outside he could see a silver statue of a girl standing on a sphere in the middle of a fountain. Her head was thrown back and her arms were tossed out to her sides. Her dress seemed to ruffle just then in a nonexistent breeze.

"An adventurous spirit, isn't she?" a deep, thick-accented voice said behind him. Markus gasped and spun about.

"I'm sorry. I didn't mean to startle you," the man said holding up his hands.

"You, you didn't," Markus said but he could feel the heat burning his cheeks.

"Who are you?" he asked the man.

"I am the conductor," the man answered and tapped his name tag.

"I need your tickets or pass, please?" the conductor asked holding out his hand.

"Of course," Markus responded, He reached into his pockets searching for his ticket hoping his mother hadn't kept it.

"Here it is."

The conductor took it, snapped it with a hole puncher then handed the ticket back.

"Where're we going anyway?" Markus asked.

"Wherever your imagination takes you," the conductor smiled and started to leave.

"Wait. What do you mean?"

"This train has but one destination; whatever you wish it to be. So, tell me," the conductor said with a wink and a smile, "Where do you wish to go?"

Markus glanced back at the statue then looked to the conductor.

"Let adventure take us where it will!" Markus said and returned the smile.

Maybe he was going to like this trip after all.

April

Nature in Chattanooga

On These Back Trails

by Jennifer Daniels Neal

The wet leaves came to smell like freedom
Freedom was the carpet of our peace
And patience creaked and groaned up in the oak trees
Which, in turn, bowed down and dropped more of their leaves

Seasons circled our back trails with forgiveness
Every bluet called it forth and made it grow
And hurled us toward the cliffs of rudimentary
Solo flight into adulthood of the soul

I will one day gather all the leaves around me
When they come to plant me down in this good soil
I will sprout inside the mercy of my childhood
And remember to forget the later toil

I will welcome heaven with the wonder
Welcoming of summer
Pouring out of schoolhouse kind of joy

May

On the Water

Martin and the Fish

by James Brumbaugh

Martin is alone on the open ocean. His vessel is too small for the journey. It is barely wider than his hips, barely longer than he is when he's laying down, not deep enough to provide any protection from the waves. But Martin makes do with what he has. He's always done so.

Blue eyes turned too pale in the unrelenting sun. Water, unbroken for miles, is that all there is. Or is that simply an image the sun has burned on his retinas? He'll never know unless the horizon changes. Martin left his home in a hurry, long ago. He hadn't been prepared for a voyage of this length. Meager items lay amongst his feet. A dull knife flecked with rust, a string, and three fourths of a rotting finger taken from his own hand.

He picks up the string and idly ties it round the finger, leans over the side of his craft and lets it plop into the water. Trying his hand as a fisherman. Fishing is a matter of patience. Waiting comes easily to a man who has spent an eternity in the sea.

His previous tries have all ended in failure. A few nibbles, but nothing solid. In his nightmares he sees his bones picked clean, his chances at a decent meal vanished into dust. When he wakes, he promises himself to eat the finger himself before letting it come to that. For now, he is content to try his luck.

Time is meaningless. Because of his position on the globe and the season, the sun is eternal. It will be months before night falls. An endless day on an endless sea, endless water and endless thirst.

A tug on the string and Martin is suddenly alert, he is a Lazarus. A wild heart is thundering in him, scorched by the sun but not yet ash. He is totally still. He is a divining rod. Martin is outside of his body, watching himself, watching the fish, watching like God. As he yanks the string he imagines that he is God, and that the fish is himself. The fish shines in the air and plops into the narrow craft with a thud. It is between Martin's legs, slimy on his calves. He drives his heel into its middle, crushes its spine. Its mouth opens and closes dumbly.

Martin stares into its black eye. It coughs like a man and is still. He takes it in his shaking hands and feels a sort of remorse. The knife is a foul tool, of little use for gutting. He winds up more ripping than cutting. Martin grabs at the innards and feels something hard and round in his hand. A coin. He dips his hands in the ocean, wipes at the viscera coating the coin. Silver, finely crafted, a portrait of the Queen. This is no mere coin, but a coin of his realm, a coin from his home.

Giggles rack his body, make him shake, make tears spring from his eyes. A coin from home. There are times at sea when one may imagine that home is a dream, that home is a fabrication, a trick, a mirage. But with this coin in hand, the boat begins to seem like a mirage, the ocean like a dream. He blesses the fish, kisses its cold mouth, blushes like a schoolgirl.

The little boat bobs like a cork in the water. There's no way to know in which direction Martin is moving, or if he's moving at all. But Martin picks the bones from the fish, examines them, thin and almost translucent, and he doesn't care where he's going. He has the fish's raw white meat, tasty after such a long famishment, and he has his coin, hot in the sun and shiny, heavy in his hand. The weight of it brings him home.

June

A Childhood Memory

Circa 1971

by Natalie Kimbell

now a skeleton of splintering plywood,
our abandoned centennial of childhood
lost to the briers, mourns

a leaning frame of kid foraged 2x4's salvaged
scraps of faded paneling pieced like a quilt teeter
underneath pieces of rusted corrugated tin

a madman's haphazard array of nails
half in, half bend over in grief
illustrate our childish mastery

we built it, my sister and I
on the edge of the yard
among winter dusted sage grass

when completed we elbow crawled
side by side scooting our puppy
Charlie Brown, ahead of us

our legs extending beyond the doggie door,
our mismatched sweats, gloves and tousled toboggans
soaked stomachs and thighs absorbing

thawing ground beneath our Taj Mahal
just us, hidden in our masterpiece of the discarded
breathing the secret satisfying smell of earth and puppy

July

Fun Fact (about Chattanooga)

The Track Nine Beam

by G. N. Zaccaria

"It's a wonder nobody got killed here tonight!" said one of the Car Men for the railroad, captivated by what had happened a few minutes earlier. "Nobody hurt?"

"Just one lady," replied the Porter. "Twisted her ankle somethin' fierce a' runnin' away as that baggage car jumped the platform. They asked if she needed a doctor but she told 'em no, she just wanted to get on her train and get back home to Cincinnati."

"Well she ain't gonna make it."

"The hell she ain't." The Engineer, standing nearby, spit a glob of chewing tobacco onto the tracks of the next platform. "I'm getting the "Special" out of here by midnight. I already called over to the boys in the Switch Tower crew. I never been late more than one hour coming out of this Terminal, and this ain't gonna slow me down. "Marked for late departure on July 17, 1953" ain't gonna be recorded on my transfer sheets. I got a Pension and a Union Card to protect."

By this time, the Station Agent had lumbered out from his office and was thundering down the platform to the men, with chest heaving and perspiration dripping from his forehead and neck.

"What about that beam?" he piped. "Look at that dent! I want to talk to you!" The Station Agent wagged his finger toward the Engineer.

"I ain't got time for small talk and silly chitter-chatter. I got me a train to move." He turned and sauntered toward the other end of the platform.

"And you! You the conductor? "How did you overshoot the end of the track? Ain't you never backed a train into Terminal Station before?"

"Nope, this is my first time coming in here. The height of the bumping post just come up on us all of a sudden."

One of the Terminal shoeshine boys ran towards the men. "Mister

Station Agent, sir. I done gots the Central on the telephone line just like you asked me, sir. They's a-holding until you gets back to your desk."

"Come with me to my office, Conductor. I need to file a report."

The two railroad men pushed through the crowd of passengers that had gathered to observe. A newspaper photographer had already arrived and was popping flashbulbs. Everyone curiously looked at the derailed baggage car, the twisted iron gates, the destroyed platform-end bumper, and at the dented support I-beam.

"Like that man asked, what about that beam? That sure don't look good at all."

"The whole roof is about to collapse!"

"No it ain't."

"It's just a little bent out of shape is all."

"How are they gonna fix an iron girder support beam that's bent like that?"

"They can do it! My Daddy can do it!" Another one of the platform Shoeshine boys stepped forward. "My daddy's on the repair crew here. He can fix anything. He says a good welder can cut out a few pieces, weld in a few new plates, get a machine to straighten some of it back up. It'll always show some being busted up, but anything can be fixed."

"Okay folks," shouted a Platform Attendant. "Please keep moving toward your designated train or into the Terminal. We have passengers and baggage moving here. Sky Caps a-coming through!"

The crowd dispersed as workers began to unload the contents of the crippled baggage car. A Switch Man uncoupled the twisted knuckle connectors of the car to prepare for the train to pull forward from the station platforms.

"Yessiree,"said the Shoeshine boy. "My daddy can have that there beam fixed by the end of the week. Anybody that walks underneath that big "Choo Choo Time" clock a-hanging over this Track Nine is gonna know that when a train car jumped the track, it was a railroad man like my Daddy who done fixed it all better again."

August

Rock City Gnome

Satisfied

by Pamela Kiper

Why should I roam like
Travelocity's gnome when
Rock City's my home?

September

Anything Cherokee

Going to Water, The Funeral of a Boy

by Jennifer Daniels Neal

"Ees, what is this place?" Banner turns full round three times. I knew he'd love it.

We drove the go-kart to get here. Well, Banner drove it—well, if you can call it that. He sped about, careening wildly to test the turning radius and nearly the roll bar as well.

Now we're on foot in this lush, green glen where the trees grow further apart than in any other area of the wood. Sunlight filters through the branches, turning everything yellow. The river is swollen, but it rolls in smooth, gentle mounds, not in turbulent, hammering falls.

"Nana used to say that it was a place like this where King David wrote the twenty-third Psalm. You know the one? 'The LORD is my shepherd?'"

"'He leads me beside quiet waters.'" Banner turns around yet again. "'He restores my soul.'"

Several stacks of large, moss-covered stones surround us. In this secluded landscape, they seem to have grown as organically as the trees, and yet there is no natural explanation for them. Banner inspects each one with his usual curiosity. He walks between them, measures the distance in steps, and finally gives his attention to me. "Burial ground?" he guesses, and he's right.

"Cherokee. Most of the Eastern Band live in North Carolina now."

I find the newest stack of rocks which is still over a decade old. "This is the grave of a little boy named Onacona. I know because I chanted his name about a million times during his funeral."

"What was that like?"

"It was long. It lasted for seven days." I search my memory for details that Banner would find intriguing and brush the tops of the tiny, white flowers that grow among the graves.

"A holy man cleansed the boy's body right here on a blanket." I show Banner where, beside the grave, the little boy was laid. "He used a lavender-scented oil and wrapped him in a white cloth."

The scent of that oil is as strong in my memory as it had been in reality, and I swear it hangs in the air now, allowing me to view the event like a photo gallery.

"The trees provided a sparse canopy, as they do today. Ferns speckled the hillside and those tiny flowers—all around where the body lay."

Before Banner can ask, I say, "No. I do not know the name of the flowers."

"How can you not know that?" he laughs.

This has become a thing. He wants me to identify every wildflower, every bulbous mushroom, every twisting tree root.

"We slept outside, at the funeral. I only went home to eat—and only then because all the mourners fasted. Nana said it would be rude to eat in front of them. But otherwise, I joined in as if I was part of the tribe. It was beautiful and eery. Prayers and songs were offered continually, even through the dark. The moon came up through the clouds like in a movie, this moment hidden, this moment revealed. And I chanted the boy's name for hours—all the women did. The men went off and came back with ashes drawn on their faces.

"On the seventh day, the holy man took us to the river where we filed in, as silent as could be. We were told to immerse ourselves seven times, lifting hands to the east and then to the west. It must have been a sight, tens of us rising from the water like we were rising from our graves. Can you imagine? They called it 'going to water,' and it was meant to release Onacona's soul to Creator. The Cherokee have no word for religion, did you know?"

He shakes his head.

"But their spirituality is built into everything. Onacona's family was given new clothes and jewelry made of sanctified stones from the river. And that was that. We cooked and ate."

October

Local Urban Legend

The Black Track Ghost of Soddy

by Laura Miller

Gather 'round, Children,
Miss Walker would say
and share some tales

of our coal mining past
with cave-in disasters and a few
ghosts, the most notorious one

along Black Track—today's Durham Street— that
was named for coal chunks fallen from railcars
rumbling from the mines to Big Soddy Creek.

The story began with a love triangle:
an unfaithful bride, a town clerk,
and a coal miner—

then, a murder
a fugitive couple
and a mysterious drowning

of the runaway bride
whose wet specter wanders
the black track

as a silent companion
with no breaths of condensation
clouds on a frigid night

Some claim she foreshadows
a dear one's death. So
beware of solitary strangers

we were warned,
and look out for tumbled
coal by the wayside.

"High Point Climbing Gym"

photograph by John C. Mannone

Author Biographies

Alexandria Kelly

Alexandria Kelly is a graduate of the University of Central Florida Creative Writing program. Originally from Mississippi, she moved to the Chattanooga area in 2019, where she lives, happily with her husband Zachary and their car Miri. She placed third in the Fiction category of the 2020 Spring Writing Contest and placed second Fiction category in the 2021 Spring Writing contest.

Amy White Ziegler

Amy lives with her husband and eight-year-old daughter in the suburbs of Chattanooga. She leads church groups and field trips, organizes play dates and closets, and makes as much time for reading and writing as this season of motherhood allows. Amy earned degrees in English from Seattle Pacific University, Western Washington University, and the University of Tennessee. After teaching college composition and literature for several years, she worked as an editor for a research center in Washington, DC. Amy has published academic articles and a piece for "The Well" online. She is currently working on her first book—a memoir about revising her adolescent conception of God.

Barbara Graham Tucker

Barbara Graham Tucker has published seven novels. She attends the Ft. Oglethorpe Northwestern Georgia Writers Group. She mentors others writers and writes short fiction when a moment or image moves her to do so. She is a professor and administrator at Dalton State College.

Daniel Rosas

Daniel A.E. Rosas Ocejo is an experienced brand marketer having worked at Fortune 500 companies and global brands ranging from Coca-Cola to Kellogg's, Johnson & Johnson and Marriott. He was born and raised in Wilmington, Delaware where when he wasn't on the soccer or lacrosse fields, he was huddled with his friends around a table scarfing down pizza while exploring vast new worlds and launching out on high-stakes adventures in the role-playing games that he is now bringing to life in his novels. He currently resides in Middle Tennessee with his wife and two children.

G. N. Zaccaria

G. N. Zaccaria is a fiction-writer, playwright, artist and performer. He holds a B.F.A. from the School of Visual Arts in New York City. He is a long-term member of the Atlanta Writers Club, PenAmerica, The Dramatists Guild and Working Title Playwrights. A recent member of the Chattanooga Writers Guild, this award-wining fiction writer is currently working on a second novel.

James Brumbaugh

James Brumbaugh lives and works in Chattanooga. He loves his wife and daughter. He grew up on the coast of the Gulf of Mexico, where he drank far too much sea water.

Jennifer Daniels Neal

Jennifer Daniels Neal is a singer/songwriter, author, and teaching artist out of Lookout Mountain, GA. Her recent novel The Locke Box and its accompanying soundtrack, Songs from The Locke Box are available now. Find out more at JenniferDaniels.com.

John DeVore

John DeVore is a teacher and writer in Hamilton County, TN.

Kathy Bowe

Kathy Bowe is an emerging writer from Chicago, currently enjoying the incredible landscapes of Chattanooga, Tennessee. She is a marketing, copywriting, and graphic design professional by day; but whenever possible, she escapes into her passion of short fiction and prose poetry. Currently, she is working on a short story collection that explores the dark side of human connections.

Laura Miller

Laura Miller is a local writer and poet who studied creative writing at the University of Tennessee at Chattanooga. A long-time teacher and community volunteer, she presently works as a legal assistant.

Mark Anderson

Mark loves the creative environment of Chattanooga and is involved with writing, music, and special events. He has been a member of the Chattanooga Writers' Guild since 2016 and has served on the Board in various roles. www.mjanderson.art

Natalie Kimbell

Natalie Kimbell lives in Sequatchie County, Tennessee. She is a mother of two, and a grandmother of four. She works as a teacher of English, creative theater, and creative writing at her high school alma mater. Her poetry is published in The 2019 Chattanooga Writers' Guild Anthology, and The 2020 Garfield Lake Review, The 2020 Chattanooga Writers' Guild Anthology, the 2021 Appalachian Writers Anthology, Dorothy Allison Version and The American Diversity Report. Her work appears in the 2021/22 Women of Appalachia Project's "Women Speak" anthology, the anthology, Beautiful: In the Eye of the Beholder, and issue 82 2022 second quarter in Abyss and Apex. Natalie also serves on the board of the Chattanooga Writer's Guild. Her nonfiction " Attention Deficit Lollapaloosa" will be published in the Chattanooga Writers Anthology for 2022.

Pamela Kiper

The Amazing Race reference in this poem comes from Pam Kiper's long-time affection for this TV series. In addition to creating some of her own versions of the Amazing Race, Pam enjoys working with kids and writing poetry and non-fiction. She has had devotionals published by the Holston Conference of the UMC but writes mostly for her own enjoyment.

Patricia Hope

Patricia Hope's award-winning writing has appeared in Chicken Soup for the Soul, Number One, Pigeon Parade Quarterly, 2021 Anthology of Appalachian Writers, The Mildred Haun Review, Liquid Imagination, American Diversity Report, and many others. She lives in Oak Ridge, Tennessee.

Sherry Poff

Sherry Poff writes in and around Ooltewah, Tennessee. She holds an M.A. in writing from The University of Tennessee at Chattanooga and is member of the Chattanooga Writers' Guild. Her work has appeared in various publications including Speckled Trout Review, Raconteur Review, Heart of Flesh, The Chattanooga Pulse and Artemis Journal and Number One.

"North Shore"

photograph by Mark Anderson

Chattanooga Writers' Guild

THE GUILD PROMOTES, **ENCOURAGES, AND SUPPORTS WRITING AND FOSTERS A** SUPPORTIVE, CARING **ENVIRONMENT** FOR WRITERS IN THE **CHATTANOOGA COMMUNITY.**

Read.
Write.
Connect.

CHATTANOOGAWRITERSGUILD.ORG

BECOME A MEMBER TODAY!

Made in the USA
Columbia, SC
19 April 2023

15573709R00054